[CODING YOUR PASSION™]

USING COMPUTER SCIENCE IN EDUCATION CAREERS

XINA M. UHL

Rosen YA™
New York

Published in 2020 by The Rosen Publishing Group, Inc.
29 East 21st Street, New York, NY 10010

First Edition

Cataloging-in-Publication Data

Names: Uhl, Xina M., author.
Title: Using computer science in education careers / Xina M. Uhl.
Description: First edition. | New York : Rosen Publishing, 2020. | Series: Coding your passion | Includes bibliographical references and index. | Audience: Grades: 7–12.
Identifiers: ISBN 9781508187080 (library bound) | ISBN 9781499467703 (pbk.)
Subjects: LCSH: Teaching—Vocational guidance—Juvenile literature. | Computer science—Vocational guidance—Juvenile literature. | Computer-assisted instruction—Juvenile literature.
Classification: LCC LB1775.U55 2020 | DDC 371.1—dc23

Manufactured in the United States of America

CONTENTS

INTRODUCTION

Education is a steadily growing career field. The US Bureau of Labor Statistics' *Occupational Outlook Handbook* reports that it is projected to grow 9 percent in the decade ending in 2026. This translates to almost nine hundred thousand jobs. Many of these jobs make use of coding skills and computer science in general.

The introduction of the computer has changed education. Today, computers are an important part of many forms of education, including those that take place in brick and mortar classrooms in schools, colleges, and universities. Once upon a time, the only way to get an education if you couldn't get to the campus was to enroll in mail-based correspondence classes. Lessons and exercises would be exchanged between students and teachers. While this form of instruction still exists in a limited capacity—such as in the armed forces—it has largely been replaced by online distance learning. Computer technology and the internet make up the majority of forms of distance learning. A related form of education called blended learning, or hybrid learning, makes use of some face-to-face learning and some online learning.

Teachers, trainers, and university instructors are on the front line when it comes to weaving computer science into their courses. While instructors may form the majority of available education and computer science career options, other positions do exist.

Technology has ushered in a new age in distance learning. Now students can participate in classes from their homes on their own schedules.

These include administrators at all levels of schools, developers of educational games, apps, and virtual reality. In addition, libraries, government organizations, institutes, and nonprofits often have educational departments that make use of sophisticated computer tools to provide learning opportunities to the general public as well as other populations. Private firms often specialize in computer science for student assessments like standardized tests.

Students who wish to pursue a career involving computer science and education have a host of options when it comes to making themselves attractive candidates in a competitive job market. Coding is a career that you can begin preparing for now, no matter your age. If you have motivation and access to the internet, whether through your own devices or through those at your school, libraries, or local organizations like the Boys and Girls Clubs of America, you have all that you need. By taking advantage of online tutorials, videos, and classes, you can teach yourself many coding skills that can benefit you when you are ready to hit the job market. Proactive effort like this is appreciated by employers, and you may find out that you enjoy the learning process.

This volume will provide numerous suggestions about preparations you can make, including clubs, camps, and internships. It will also offer you information about the varied needs of educational organizations and real-life educators who make use of computer science in their careers.

CHAPTER ONE

UNDERSTANDING COMPUTER SCIENCE

Computer science refers to the study of computers and the systems related to them. It deals mostly with software and the design, theory, development, and application of software. Knowing how to program, or code, is just one part of computer science. It also refers to the study of algorithms, or the step-by-step methods of problem solving. There are many branches of computer science, including programming, computer graphics, artificial intelligence, and software engineering. As computers become ever more important, this list grows more extensive.

THE EARLY DAYS

In 1833, an English inventor named Charles Babbage came up with the design for the first computer, called the Analytical Engine. Since electricity had not yet

Computer programming language, or source code, instructs devices to perform certain actions. Coding is one of the most useful skills you can acquire.

been discovered, it was mechanical, not electronic. Babbage's design included more than fifty thousand moving parts. People would provide the computer with instructions by entering punch cards into the machine.

This complex device never went beyond the design stage. An English mathematician named Ada Lovelace is called the first programmer because she created several programs for Babbage's Analytical Engine. She also developed the concept of looping, or the repetition of a series of instructions. Although the Analytical Engine never became a functioning computer, it did pave the way for later developments.

The first electronic computers were invented during the 1940s. They made use of electronic switching devices called vacuum tubes instead of mechanical parts. During World War II (1939–1945), dedicated research took place to provide British cryptographers with machines to help break enemy German communication codes. One of these cryptographers was Alan Turing. After the war's end, he helped to design an input-output system and programs for the world's first working digital computer. Around this same time, an engineer named Claude Shannon helped with the development of binary programming. A bit, or binary digit, makes up the computer's most basic unit of information. Binary codes are a series of 1s and 0s. When arranged into patterns, these bits tell computers to perform certain actions.

These early computer punch cards date from around 1970. They were fed into huge mainframe computers.

Just as Charles Babbage had envisioned, binary codes were fed into computers with punch cards.

Circuit boards could also communicate with computers when a series of wires were inserted and unplugged. These early computers were expensive, heavy, and large enough to fill up entire rooms. Transistors replaced unreliable vacuum tubes in 1947. The development of an integrated circuit in 1958 helped to make computers much smaller. The microprocessor, invented in 1971, allowed computers to become even smaller and lighter.

Though binary code made up the basis for computer instructions, it was slow and difficult to work with. Programming languages made it easier to code by using words or phrases to create common computer instructions. The first high-level programming language, developed in 1947, is called FORTRAN. COBOL, developed in the early 1960s, became an important language for business uses. Other early languages include BASIC and C. C++ came about in the mid-1980s, and a simplified version of it called Java debuted in the 1990s.

Programs as they are written do not always work perfectly. When they need to be fixed, the process is known as debugging. This is an essential step in the coding process.

Most early computer systems used specially customized hardware and software. Microsoft created an operating system in the 1980s. Called Windows, it interfaced with computer codes in a more user-friendly manner.

As computers grew in popularity, different languages have been developed to create programs specific to each industry. Software developers came up with web browsers such as Microsoft's Internet Explorer to more easily navigate the internet.

COMPUTERS AND EDUCATION: A BRIEF HISTORY

Since the mid-twentieth century, computers have risen steadily in popularity and have made their way into almost every industry. This includes government, business, and education. In 1944, the first computer at Harvard University replaced the slide rule (a device used for complex calculations). The earliest courses of study to use computers were science, engineering, and mathematics. In 1963, Stanford University introduced computer-assisted instruction to help students of math and reading take drills and practice concepts.

In the 1970s, a scholar at Massachusetts Institute of Technology (MIT), Seymour Papert, developed a programming language called LOGO. It was designed to help children learn mathematics in a different way than children had previously. Eventually, Papert began to use LOGO to work with LEGO construction kits. The idea is that students learn better when defining problems and using their problem-solving skills to solve them.

By 1974, more than two million students used computers in their classes. By the end of the 1970s, computers had become standard in higher education. The number of students using computers has only grown over the last few decades. A 2008 survey by the National Center for Education Statistics (NCES) found that 100 percent of public

(continued on the next page)

(continued from the previous page)

schools had at least one computer for student use. The ratio of students to computers used for instruction was three to one.

Computer usage in education must keep up with trends in the business world as well as at home. A 2015 NCES survey reports that public school students with their own or a shared digital device at home was 95 percent of fourth graders, 98.3 percent of eighth graders, and 98 percent of twelfth graders. With statistics like that, computers and education will have a strong relationship for the foreseeable future.

ARE YOU CUT OUT TO CODE?

The most recent developments in computer technology have made devices smaller and more portable than ever. Desktop personal computers (PCs), whether Macs or Windows-based, are widely available in businesses and public organizations such as libraries and universities. But the home use of smaller devices such as laptops, tablets, and smartphones continues to grow ever more popular. Each of these devices uses computer coding, providing programmers with more opportunities than ever to practice and create programs, apps, games, and more.

Certain skills and traits distinguish coders from the rest of the world. Let's take a look at what those are. Coders need the ability to think logically since programming works on the assumption that a solution to a task exists. Logical thinking also helps to break down an action into the smaller steps needed to perform it. Creativity helps coders figure out unusual approaches to problem solving. Persistence is necessary because coding is often trial and error. It can be easy to grow frustrated when the results wanted are slow in coming, so patience is also a must. An enduring interest in problem solving will help to get through the sometimes-tedious work of successful coding. Perhaps you feel confident that you have each of these attributes. Perhaps you aren't as patient or creative as you would like. Don't worry, you will have plenty of opportunities to practice and develop these skills.

CODING WITH OTHERS AND ON YOUR OWN

If you find that you do better with the structure of in-person events or classes, there are plenty of those available. One event that takes place every December is the Hour of Code. It lasts only one hour and serves as a quick introduction to computer science. For those who find coding intimidating, it is a simple way to show that computer basics can be learned by anyone. Chances are there is an Hour of Code event near you, maybe even in your school, since thousands occur worldwide every year.

If you're interested in a summer tech camp, take a look at what iD Tech has to offer. Located in twenty-nine states, its camps include coding, design, and robotics. Each camp is designed for young people aged seven through eighteen. The 2,700 US locations of the YMCA also offer summer technology camps.

Many people rely on taking classes to learn job skills. There's nothing wrong with that. But computer coding can be learned on your own, provided you have internet access, some motivation, and a willingness to learn as you go.

Hundreds of computer languages have developed over recent decades, but certain languages have risen in popularity. Freecodecamp.org has analyzed

Learning by doing, or coding on your own and with others, is the most powerful form of computer education.

the best computer languages to learn to put you on a well-paying career path. The top ten are JavaScript, Swift (for Apple iOS or macOS), Python, Java, C++, Ruby (designed to be beginner friendly and easy to use), Rust, Elixir, Scala, and R. The easiest languages to get started using are Ruby and Python. Freecodecamp.org is a great site to start your coding journey. Sign-up is free and allows you to participate in more than 1,400 coding challenges, to build up to thirty projects, and to earn up to six certifications. Along the same lines is Codecademy, which offers both free and paid options to learn coding. Millions have taken advantage of the courses.

One means of learning the coding language Ruby is to try the tool Hackety Hack. It's a great choice for absolute beginners. Beginner apps for the iPad are Hopscotch, Tynker, and Move the Turtle, which make learning coding fun. Scratch is a web-based language and visual coding system that makes easy apps and games. Robotics can be learned with Arduino Programming Language, which is built on C++, or Lego Mindstorms NXT.

Google's Blockly project works by using blocks in the shape of puzzle pieces to create computer programs. The blocks snap together to create a program without the need to type on a keyboard. When one puzzle is mastered, another provides more advanced challenges until eventually the student switches to regular text-based programming.

If you'd like to jump into creating your own app instead, you can access a variety of software development kits (SDKs) online.

CHAPTER TWO

TEACHERS AND TECH

Teachers fill around three million positions across the United States, at all different levels and for all different subjects. They teach at public and private schools, colleges, and universities. Their working hours usually take place during the day when students are in session, though they often work grading papers and preparing lessons at nights and on weekends. Some teachers at colleges and universities may hold classes at night or during the weekend. Depending on whether the school they work at is in session year round or not, teachers may or may not work during the summer months.

K–12 TEACHERS

The main types of schoolteachers are those who teach elementary school (from the start of school—usually

Classroom teachers are an invaluable source of early, intermediate, and advanced computer learning. In-person instruction is necessary for most learners at some time.

kindergarten—through fifth grade), middle school teachers (sixth through eighth grades), and high school teachers (ninth through twelfth grades). Their job growth outlook through the decade ending in 2026 is about 8 percent per year, about as fast as average job growth. This amounts to about 250,000 new jobs through 2026.

Except for teachers at some private schools, schoolteachers must possess a bachelor's degree and pass a state-issued certification or license. They may need to have coursework in the subject they will be teaching. Also, a background check may be required. Some important qualities for teachers are:

- **Good communication skills**. In addition to interacting with students, teachers need to work with other teachers and to communicate student needs to school administrators and parents.
- **Patience.** Teachers must work with students of varying abilities and different backgrounds, requiring them to be able to remain calm and supportive at all times.
- **Stamina.** Keeping up physical, mental, and emotional strength when dealing with kindergartners, elementary students, and middle school students is important.
- **Resourcefulness.** Teachers must work to explain difficult concepts so that students can understand. They also must command students' attention.

MUSIC EDUCATION AND COMPUTERS

Brian Stiffler, who holds a doctorate in music education, has a wide range of experience teaching music. He has led band programs in the Midwest and Germany and taught a number of music courses at universities such as the University of Southern Mississippi and the University of Illinois. He describes one meaningful experience here:

> ***I was teaching in Ramstein, Germany, at the US air base, in the middle of an after-school clarinet lesson, when [the terrorist attacks on] 9/11 happened. It had a great effect on me, being so far from home. I used my skills as a musician and an educator to compose the Ramstein Reflections to deal with it. The different sections had different associations. The first section represented the time before 9/11; the second represented the time during the disaster; the third section represented the US military response, Operation Enduring Freedom. I incorporated woodwinds, brass, and percussion. After each section, we would stop and discuss the things that had happened and how the music represented them. It was a great learning experience for my students.***
>
> ***One of the trumpet players at our school was a Muslim. The other students did not know***

(continued on the next page)

(continued from the previous page)

> ***how to treat him following 9/11, whether his religion promoted violence against them. The trumpeter's father came by and talked to the class so they could learn more about his faith. That, also, was a good learning experience for the whole class.***

Stiffler's band performed the Ramstein Reflections for an audience several times. As he composed the original work, he made use of Finale music notation software to enter parts for individual instruments. Finale gave him the ability to review and edit the music as he went along. Finale also allowed him to print out parts for each student and to play audio examples of the piece during class instruction.

COLLEGE AND UNIVERSITY INSTRUCTORS

Teachers beyond the high school level are also known as postsecondary teachers. They work at colleges, universities, community or junior colleges, and professional schools. They are specialists in their subject, such as computer science, education, health, and so on. Their job growth outlook through the decade ending in 2026 is about 15 percent per year, much faster than average. This amounts to about two

University of Pennsylvania professor Peter Struck and his teaching assistant teach an online mythology class from Philadelphia. Online courses have skyrocketed in popularity over the last decade.

hundred thousand new jobs through 2026. Much of this growth will be in part-time positions.

Most postsecondary instructors must have doctorates, or PhDs, though community colleges may require only a master's degree in the field of expertise. Instructors must have a license, certification, or registration if they are teaching subjects that will be granted these credentials. One example is a nursing instructor who would need a nursing license to teach in a nursing program.

Postsecondary instructors must communicate well and be resourceful, just like teachers of younger students. Other important qualities are:

- **Critical-thinking skills.** These are necessary to conduct research and design experiments in a logical manner.
- **Verbal skills.** Since instructors must give lectures, they must possess good verbal, or speaking, skills.
- **Writing skills.** Since instructors need to publish original research and analysis, they must have the ability to write clearly.

THE SKINNY ON TECH AND TEACHING

Everyone in education seems to be concerned about technology in the classroom, including President Donald Trump. A presidential memorandum issued on September 25, 2017, provides a minimum of $200 million per year toward increasing students' access to science, technology, engineering, and mathematics (STEM) in education. The focus of the memo is computer science. The memo states:

> ***Despite overwhelming evidence that coding skills and STEM literacy will be critical to***

achieving high-paying jobs of the future, too few schools across the country are able to provide students with high-quality education and training in STEM and computer science. Fewer than half of America's high schools offer computer programming instruction. Women, minorities, and students in rural communities often have even lower participation in STEM education, and will benefit from the efforts that this PM sets into motion.

More than five hundred thousand computing jobs are available each year, but only fifty thousand American students graduate with computer science degrees each year, showing the gap in public schools' computer science education. A 2017 study conducted by SAM Labs, an educational and coding company, says that 82 percent of US teachers report that technology is critical to prepare students for the job market. Math and science are the most tech-intensive subjects in school, but teachers have reported that technology is helpful in the study of reading and writing, English literature, and history as well.

Another study by Edgenuity reports that schools fall short in their use of technology in the classroom. Sixteen percent of teachers give their schools an A for the technology their students have available while 53 percent give their schools a B and 31 percent feel as though their schools rate a C through F.

FOCUSING ON COMPUTERS

Like a blackboard and chalk, computers provide ways for teachers to show information to students as a class or group. They allow teachers to communicate with students quickly by email and enter grades online so that students and parents can follow a student's progress. But they can do much more than that.

GETTING SOCIAL

Social media like Twitter, Facebook, Instagram, and others allow students and teachers with the tools to interact, collaborate, and communicate. Teachers use them in all kinds of creative ways to bring learning and value to their classrooms. Some examples include posting status updates as a class, writing blog posts about current lessons, getting feedback on science fair projects, and having students host a video series or podcast. The uses are endless. Not only do social media help students get excited about learning, but they also extend into the business world as an important job skill. Teachers can also make use of social media to access learning networks and participate in their own career development by identifying resources available and learning about teaching techniques.

DIGITAL GRADEBOOKS AND MORE

Classroom management apps, specialized software, and other tools are bringing computer science into

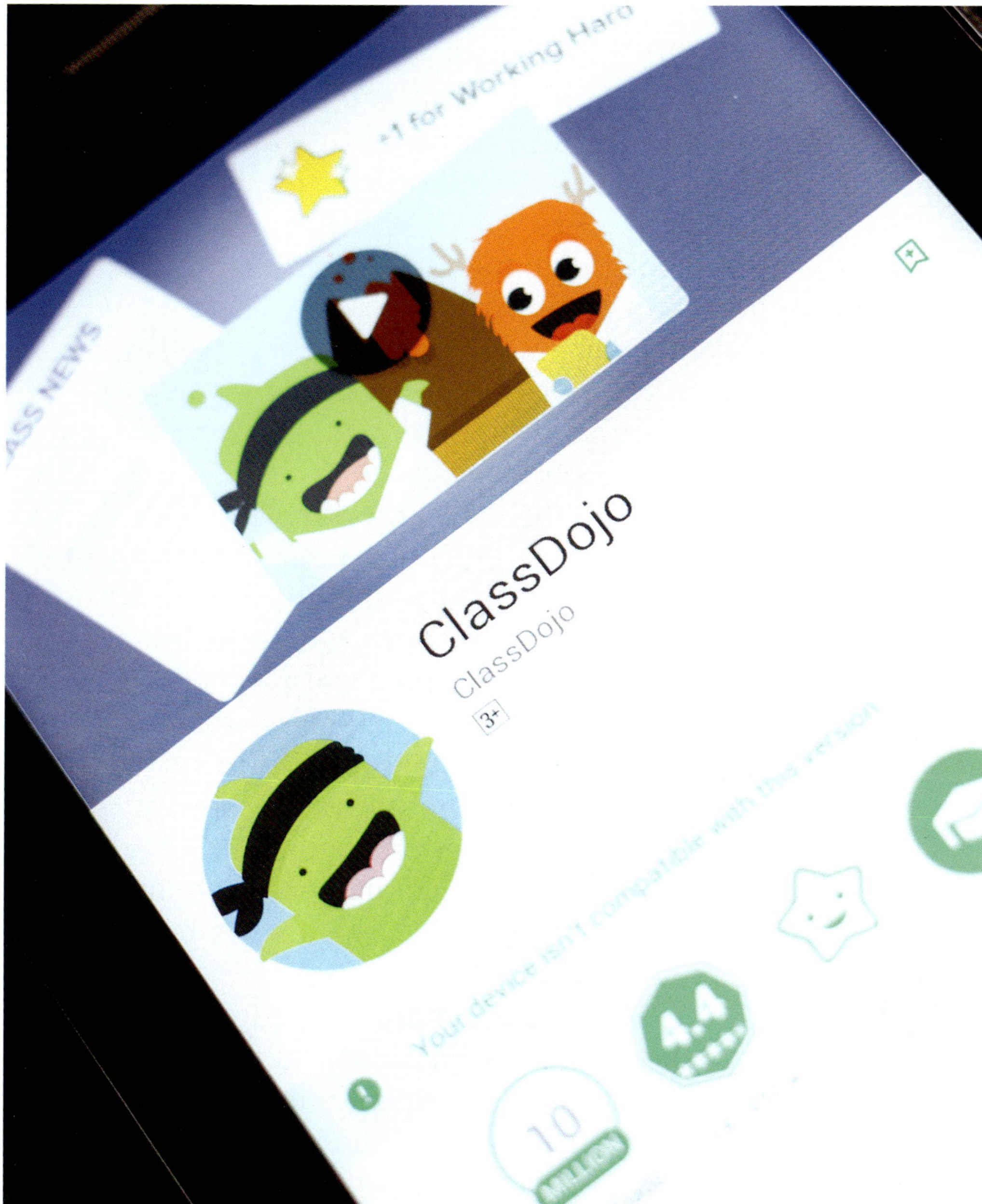

A popular app used in classrooms today is ClassDojo. It helps teachers encourage students to behave in a positive manner while allowing parents and teachers to communicate.

schools in a big way. ClassDojo is a popular, fun app primarily used for K–8 schools. It rewards students for positive behavior and penalizes them for negative behavior and shares information about students with their parents. Available for the operating systems iOS, Android, Kindle Fire, and Windows or MacOS, it includes multiple features such as classroom directions to keep students on track; music designed to help students focus or have fun; a noise meter that helps students know when to quiet down; a group organizer that arranges students into pairs, threes, and other groups; and other features.

NetSupport School calls itself a complete classroom management solution. It allows teachers to monitor students' desktops or devices in real time, to demonstrate presentations and other lesson material, to design and administer tests and quizzes, and more. MySchoolWorx offers multiple uses as well, giving teachers and administrators a portal to communicate with students, and allowing parents to access student grades, homework, and behavior and attendance reports. Parents can also pay for tuition and other events and even order lunches. It's available for smartphones, tablets, and laptops.

Gameification allows teachers to create games of quiz and test questions and rewards students with a sense of accomplishment when they answer correctly. It's used in some software like Socrative. Stick Pick is an assessment app that encourages student participation.

Google products are popular in the classroom, just as they are in the business world and for personal

Google Classroom is free for all users. This app provides a central point for teachers and students to communicate, distribute assignments, and organize classwork.

use. Google Docs provides free, easy-to-use word processor, spreadsheet, and presentation programs that allow students to save their work to access from anywhere and to collaborate on assignments.

Google Classroom has tools for K–12 and for postsecondary, or higher, education. It works with Chromebooks, or inexpensive, simple laptops that use the Chrome web browser instead of Windows. It also makes use of tools for announcements, to give quizzes and tests, to assign homework, and to give out grades. Digital tools are available to allow students to make videos, record podcasts, and practice coding. Administrators, teachers, students, and parents alike benefit from Google Classroom.

A few other programs that teachers make use of include Class Charts, a digital seating chart system that also rewards students for good behavior and participation; Handouts, a paperless system for worksheets that is especially good for elementary teachers; and Bloomz for parent-teacher communication. For instructors at higher levels, Peergrade is a feedback tool with high-quality rubrics.

TECH ON SCHOOL GROUNDS

The California Board of Education is ahead of the game when it comes to helping students learn coding skills. They have focused on using lessons that make use of computers in varied ways. Los Angeles Unified School District (LAUSD) created the Instructional Technology Initiative to help teachers learn ways to help students with computer instruction. This effort has resulted in a 76 percent increase in middle and high school student enrollment in computer science programming courses. Middle schools offer introductory classes, game design, and app development. High school courses include more advanced courses like web development, cybersecurity, and robotics. High school students can also take Advanced Placement computer science for college credit.

One example of using tech in the classrooms involves GIS (geographic information system). It's a way of looking at locations and putting layers of information over maps and 3D scenes. This helps users to identify patterns, effects, and relationships they might not see otherwise. Graphing information can help students deepen their understanding of their lessons.

ArcGIS is a platform that uses GIS in the classroom. Examples of ways it provides learning include a map of the northern American colonies with its religious makeup to make it clear to students how many religions existed—and where—in the colonies at the time of the novel *The Scarlet Letter*. A map used to study another novel, *The Red Badge of Courage*, shows cities, bodies of water, and other locations mentioned in the book. Mathematics can be taught by creating a map that shows the volume of an Egyptian pyramid. Another use is to produce a map that shows how population numbers in the United States have changed over time. The uses for maps as teaching tools can be endless, limited only by the users' creativity.

CHAPTER THREE

CODE IN THE CLASSROOM

In the 1980s and 1990s, increased access to computers and the internet brought a new dimension to teaching. Teachers and students could now use web-based tools to communicate through web conferences, television videos or channels, online bulletin boards, and email. Students who lived in remote areas, who worked during the day, or who had schedules that did not allow them to go to a traditional school now did not have to attend classes in physical locations. Instead, they could do so from their homes or other places at whatever time they chose.

THE VIRTUAL CLASSROOM

Distance teaching is now mostly online learning. Some students attend completely online. Others opt for blended learning, which allows students to take both on-campus and online classes at the same time. How

Virtual classrooms provide learners with video, audio, email, and forum-based communication between teachers and students. The idea is to engage learners in their own education.

much of the instruction takes place online depends on the course. This means that some classes may have about 30 percent of their material online while others might have up to 70 percent online.

In higher education, students report that they find blended learning courses more engaging than traditional classrooms. However, universities can take this concept too far in an effort to save on costs. Students at the University of Central Florida's College of Business objected to a 2018 proposal to reduce face-to-face time with instructors. Up to 30 hours weekly had previously been available but the school changed that to only 6.25 hours weekly. In-person instruction remains an important part of the learning experience for many.

Online instructors perform many of a traditional instructor's duties, but they make use of email, message boards, and other tools to connect to their students. In higher education, these instructors need a PhD, though occasionally they can get by with just a master's degree. They may also need licenses or certifications. The job outlook for this career is the same for classroom teachers, slated to grow about 8 percent for K–12 teachers and 15 percent for higher-education teachers through 2026.

Online instructors may make use of web conferencing tools like Skype, Google Hangouts, Zoom, and Adobe Connect. These programs make use of computer screens, webcams, microphones, and phones for presentations that occur in real time. All participants can interact with one another and share their screens. Other forms of technology used are prerecorded lecture videos by instructors, podcasts, audio recordings, and discussion forums. Audio for podcasts and sound files can be recorded and mixed using the free, open-source software Audacity for Mac and PC. Various plug-ins are available to customize Audacity for different operating systems. Coding skills allow users to create their own plug-ins for Audacity by using the Nyquist programming language, too.

K–12 ONLINE

Students at the elementary school, middle school, and high school levels have a variety of reasons for preferring online schooling. Some students may be homeschooled, have special needs, or just find that virtual schools suit them better. Accredited Schools Online has an online quiz to help parents decide whether their child would benefit from a virtual school. The questions make it clear that online education requires that students have reliable times and places for schoolwork, help from parents, and regular communication with teachers.

Two of the largest virtual schools are Connections Academy and K12. Connections Academy operated in twenty-five states and served more than forty-five thousand students during the 2017–2018 school year. Connections often partners with school districts to provide a customized school experience. K12 is another virtual school. It offers both fully online and blended learning options. Both schools are accredited and may be free of charge, depending on the student's location. Virtual schools like these may be public, charter, or private.

Technology provides teachers the means to personalize lessons or make them particular to the student's needs. Students can spend more time on challenging subjects and less on easier ones. Feedback can be instant and used to help students target their weak areas. Teachers contact the students face to face with online chats. Teachers

Students with health challenges that would previously have kept them out of the classroom entirely can now make use of online schools to continue their education.

may be able to work from home or show up at in-person facilities.

PLUSES AND MINUSES

Online schooling has both positives and negatives for teachers and students. The pros include the ability to monitor class performance and grades. Class files and other resources are located on computers so they are easy to access. The hours are flexible.

The cons include minimal interaction with peers and limited or no in-person contact with teachers. This kind of schooling can require more time and effort than a traditional school due to the increased need to communicate with teachers via email and through discussion forums.

TEACHER DIANE

When Diane graduated from college, she decided to move to Brazil. There, she taught English for six months. After that, she moved to Chicago, where she taught English for two years at an international language school. She soon decided to travel again and spent six months each in Ecuador and Thailand. She made a living by starting her own online business. She created a website and used Skype to conduct teaching sessions with her students. During an interview with teachingeslonline.com she said:

> ***At first I was very hesitant because one of the reasons I enjoy teaching is the personal interaction of teaching, the one-on-one direct contact with people. This is one of the best parts of teaching. But I gave it a try ... and realized that I could do even more on the internet than I could do in the classroom. I could share my screen: I use a board that I write on to screen share so it's as if I am using***

(continued on the next page)

(continued from the previous page)

> ***the classroom white board and in addition I can send links to websites. I can see what my student is doing on their screen and it feels just like real interaction.***

Diane draws her own lesson cartoons using a tablet called Wacom that she shares with students. She makes use of LinkedIn, Twitter, and other social media. By using QuickTime Player and iMovie on her Mac, she records videos for repetitive concepts and uploads them to YouTube. Coders can make use of an SDK with a license from Apple, and use QuickTime to create their own programs.

Diane's business has expanded since she opened it in 2013. Several teachers now work for her. She plans to develop other teaching websites in the future, proving that coding combines nicely with education in cyberspace.

THE WORLD AS A CLASSROOM

One of the hottest new offerings in distance education is the use of massive open online courses (MOOCs). These courses are offered online to a worldwide audience. There is no limit to the number of students who can participate. The instructor of a MOOC uses readings, video lectures, and homework problems to conduct the course. User forums encourage participation between instructors, students, and teaching assistants. The forums also offer immediate feedback on assignments, quizzes, and tests.

FutureLearn is one platform that offers MOOCs. Courses are delivered one part at a time and can be accessed on smartphones, tablets, and desktops. FutureLearn has partnered with almost 150 universities, libraries, and cultural institutions around the world. Since launching the platform in 2013, more than eight million learners have joined. Most of the courses they offer last between six and ten weeks, though some are as short as two weeks. Subjects vary widely. Sample courses are "Understanding Depression and Low Mood in Young People," "The Book of Kells: Exploring an Irish Medieval Masterpiece," and "Causes of Human Disease: Transmitting and Fighting Infection." Numerous coding courses are also available. MOOCs are free, but a certificate of achievement and unlimited access to the course is available for a fee of around $75.

For students and instructors both, there are pros and cons to the MOOC format. Pros include it being free or low cost; not having set in-class hours so students can study on a flexible schedule (though the MOOC provider usually releases one lesson per week); overcrowding not being an issue and enrollment unlimited; online quiz and testing features designed to help students keep up; and being available worldwide.

Cons include the difficulty in having meaningful conversations in this class environment, though message boards and chat rooms mean that students can help one another learn; grading papers is also not currently possible, though software is being developed to meet this challenge; and, of course, information is condensed and watered down, making it unlikely that students will understand the subject the same way that someone who took a normal quarter- or semester-long course would.

Massachusetts Institute of Technology (MIT) offers 2,400 courses as MOOCs. Their courses have attracted three hundred million visitors so far. MOOCs are offered as part of MIT's Open Learning initiative. Other popular sources of MOOCs are edX, Udemy, and Coursera.

Most MOOCs are taught by university professors at accredited universities. Open-source courses and software allow students to have opportunities to learn on their own and practice skills that could provide them with valuable experience for their résumés.

In ancient times, clay or wax tablets were used for writing. Today, students can use computer tablets to learn.

However, online courses through MOOCs do not replace a university degree in many cases. Instead, they serve as additions to traditionally learned subjects, or upgrades to keep skills fresh. Many people take MOOCs just for fun. While it is possible to obtain certificates, most employers put less stock in them than in other degrees. Coding is a frequent offering at MOOCs and can be helpful in learning new languages and techniques. Keep in mind that MOOCs are best used as an addition to other forms of education. To find available courses check with providers of MOOCs, such as MIT, edX, and so on, or visit a directory of courses from difference sources at MOOC List.

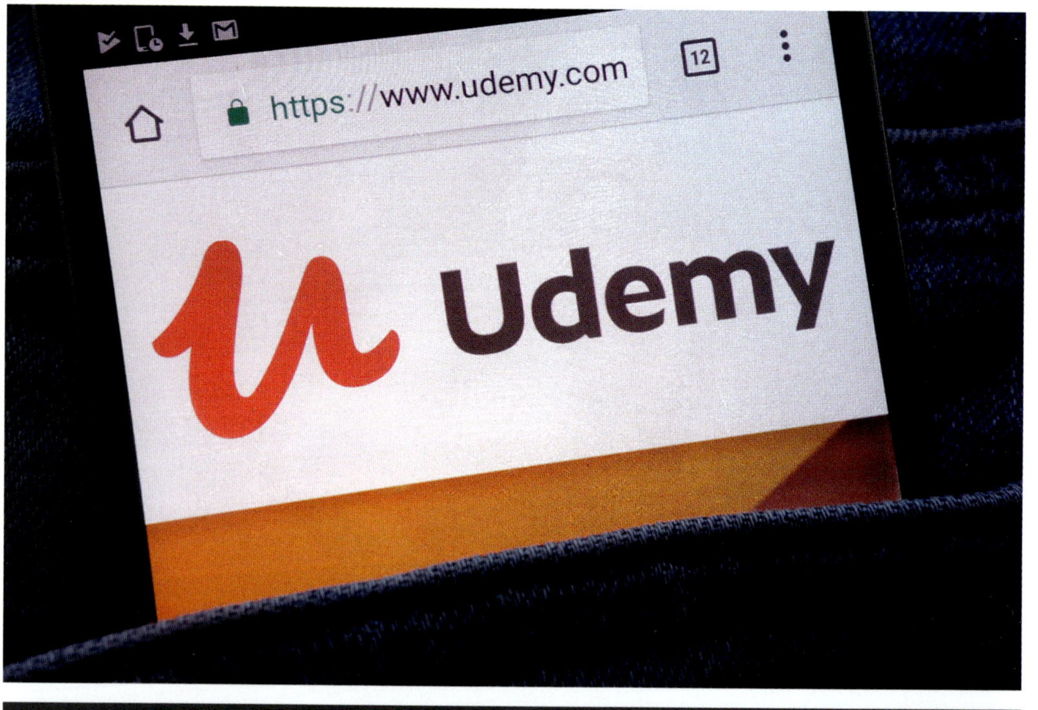

A popular source of massive online open courses (MOOCs), Udemy offers eighty thousand courses to more than twenty-four million students. MOOCs are free or a fraction of the cost of in-person courses.

What about creating the courses themselves? Perhaps you want to teach one yourself. If that is the case, visit Google's Open Online Education. Their Online Course Kit helps teachers plan the course by defining the objectives and narrowing down the specific subject; create course content, including videos, slides, documents, activities, quizzes, and tests; deliver the course to students online through the use of Google's Course Builder, an open-source platform; and communicate with students. Coding skills will help you change and customize the look, feel, and content of your course.

CHAPTER FOUR

INNOVATION IN SCHOOL ADMINISTRATION

Administrators make up a significant number of employees in elementary schools, high schools, middle schools, and other educational programs at juvenile centers, day care centers, and more. These jobs can be high level and pay well, such as superintendents, principals, vice principals, or consultants. The jobs can involve varying levels of skills in computer science.

Principals manage the daily operation of schools. They serve as bosses for teachers and other staff members and help choose the courses of study offered by the schools. Though it depends on the size of the school and whether it is public or private, principals may use various computer programs to analyze data such as student test scores and attendance and budgets.

Computer programs are used to figure out class schedules and oversee them. A principal must have at least several years of experience as a teacher and

School principals require the skills and knowledge of a teacher in addition to a talent for administration. Nowadays, an understanding of tech may also be part of the job.

a master's degree, usually in education, to qualify for the job. Principals must have all the skills of a teacher and more: critical-thinking skills to analyzing student test results and procedures; decision-making skills for the overall operation of the school and staff members; and leadership skills to motivate teachers and staff and to set goals for them. Through 2026, the job outlook is slated to grow 8 percent, or as fast as average.

While public schools usually call the top administrator a principal, private schools may call them program directors or headmasters. At the university and college level, these administrators are called department heads, deans, or provosts. In larger school districts, vice principals, assistant principals, or associate principals may take on some of the principal's workload. Experience as a vice principal is often a stepping-stone to a later promotion to principal.

THE AMAZING WORLD OF EDTECH

Jeff Herb from Lombard, Illinois, spent four years teaching English and one year directing his school's media center before he took on the challenge of becoming an associate principal. One of his strengths was in EdTech, or educational technology. Herb saw the potential for EdTech to help instruct students with different needs. Students who quickly master content, those who need extra help with the lesson material, and students in between the two extremes can all be helped when computer technology is used to customize lessons for each instance.

EdTech uses a number of different tools, such as images, text, animation, videos, and audio. It makes learning more engaging for students. Herb started a website called Instructional Tech Talk to give educators information on how to use technology in the classroom. In his job as associate principal, one of Herb's duties is to bring computer technology into the school.

Herb has great enthusiasm for using technology in the classroom. However, a lot of teachers don't share that enthusiasm: an article by *EdTech: Focus on K–12* cited a survey of two thousand K–12 teachers. Only 10

Educational technology, or EdTech, refers to software and other technology designed to improve student learning.

percent of the teachers felt confident in their abilities to bring higher-level tech into their classrooms. Teachers want a lot of training that sometimes isn't available where they work. Administrators can help teachers to adopt technology with the help of a new program by Google called the Dynamic Learning Project (DLP). The project shows principals how to use coaches and hands-on training to help teachers master technology, which they can then pass along to their students. Often with the use of DLP, teachers and students can learn alongside one another. McGuffy Middle School in Claysville, Pennsylvania, used DLP to improve grading using Google Forms, help literature students blog about class content, learn Python, and create digital art projects.

Administrators set a school's policies, and they can encourage teachers to make tech learning a priority. One way administrators can help further this goal is to create flipped classrooms. The concept was made popular by two Colorado high school chemistry teachers. They bought software to allow them to record lessons for absent students and posted them online. Soon, the teachers found that absent students weren't the only ones using the lessons. Other students were using them before class to get a head start on the class. Rather than making the class focus on a teacher giving out information that students have never encountered, a flipped class instead uses class time to work through problems and teach by doing. The idea caught fire and continues to affect classrooms across the country.

A PROGRAMMER WITH A PASSION

When Liz Ruiz got her first job out of college, she had no idea that it would lead to a career in education. Fresh from earning a Bachelor of Science degree in business administration with an emphasis in information systems, Ruiz started working in the data center of a private law school. She worked with the admissions office to process reports. Her next job was at a community college. From there, she went to Los Angeles Unified School District

(LAUSD) where she started as a programmer in the geographic information system, or GIS, department, which worked with all sorts of geographical data that corresponded with locations on the earth. Ruiz explains her work:

> ***I was in the data center where I worked with the admissions office to process reports. Eventually I moved to the GIS department. Rather than line-by-line coding, this resulted in maps rather than reports. I worked with a lot of different departments. One was the transportation department, which needed to bus students to magnet schools that focused on certain subjects such as computer science, the arts, zoology, and so on. I helped build maps to determine who would be eligible for bussing. This first involved creating maps of the walk radius of each school, or the area closest to the school where the students would be expected to walk to school. Those students that fell outside of this radius were eligible to be bused in. Maps (done by myself and others) were presented at the Board of Education meetings for the superintendent and board members.***

For students interested in GIS, Ruiz recommends that they take classes in cartography, mapmaking, math, databases, GUI, Python, and JavaScript. She also encourages students to try to get into the education industry somehow.

USING SOFTWARE FOR ADMINISTRATION

A number of software systems help school administrators run their operations efficiently. Alma provides a student information system that includes different functions: admissions, registration, enrollment, scheduling, attendance, report cards, and grading of certain standards created by government education departments. iGradePlus has many features for teachers, schools, and entire districts. These features include custom reports; communication

Like pencil sharpeners and desks, computers have become part of the necessary equipment for today's learners. Even instructors have gone paperless, meaning that all work is done digitally.

between students, parents, and the school; grades; and attendance counts. Sawyer is good for schools as well as after-school programs, camps, and classes. It includes payment processing, registration, scheduling, and communication with parents.

MAESTRO SIS by BocaVox is used by a variety of medium to large school districts, charter schools, colleges, universities, and continuing education programs. MAESTRO SIS has the capability to work for brick and mortar schools as well those that use online and blended classes. It automates administrative tasks by providing online calendars, the ability to take online payments, a bookstore management feature, bill-paying and payment-receiving capabilities, and the ability to set up class schedules. MAESTRO SIS provides tools for analytics, or systems to analyze data or statistics such as the number of students who attend and are absent on a daily basis.

THE BEGINNING OF ALMA

An interview with Jack Macleod, president of school and classroom management software company Alma, describes how the company started. They listened to teachers complain about the software available to them. Macleod and his partners started on a six-month-long research phase to learn more.

(continued on the next page)

(continued from the previous page)

After interviewing hundreds of teachers, the team at Alma came up with a list of weaknesses in other classroom management software at the time. Macleod tells EdTech Times: "After defining the problem, we built a prototype and had ten schools test it over the course of a year. After a year's worth of feedback, we honed in [sic] on the exact solution." The company worked to combine student information to be in one place on the internet (cloud computing). They also tried to make it easier to use than other software while providing schools more value at a better price.

Macleod has advice for other coders interested in entering the EdTech market: "You have to believe in what you are doing and want to make a difference in the lives of educators and students. The educators have this belief and commitment, and are wary of those who don't."

Edsby is made for school districts and provides course planning, analytics, assessments (quizzes and tests), the ability to run reports, and more.

Professors, teachers, and instructors may make up the face of classrooms, but they are only a part of those staff members who keep a school, college, or university up and running. The US Department of Education reported that in fall 2015, postsecondary institutions employed about 43,000 librarians, curators, and archivists, 204,000 business and financial operations staff, and 441,000 people in office and administrative duties. This is around 18 percent of the total number of employees (including faculty, maintenance, and other staff members). In short: that's a lot of people. Many of these staff members fall under the category of administration. They make use of a variety of computer skills to create financial reports and budgets (spreadsheets like Microsoft Excel), image presentations (Microsoft PowerPoint), and databases (Microsoft Access).

Coding skills can be especially helpful when working with databases, or organized collections of data. While Microsoft Access allows you to create and share apps without being a software developer, you may need to use customized software that you can develop in house. Coding skills allow you to extract data using database languages like Oracle, SQL SERVER, and MySQL.

CHAPTER FIVE

CODING APPS, GAMES, VR, AND MORE

There's one thing that all the software mentioned in this volume so far has in common: coders. Programmers and software developers had a hand in creating them. If you decide that working as a teacher or administrator isn't up your alley, but educational software development is, the best way to learn about software and mobile apps is to find out more about the companies that create them. By studying businesses and learning about the products they create, you can get a good idea about what they specialize in. Be sure to click on and read the About Us page on their websites so that you can learn about the company culture, or the personality of the company—what its management values and tries to accomplish. Of course, you will want to check out the Careers page as well because that will tell you what jobs are open, what they pay, and what is expected of the employee.

Think big when it comes to using your passion for coding and education in the work world. Jobs exist in coding outside of schools in private industries such as educational games.

THE CODERS BEHIND THE SOFTWARE

According to the Bureau of Labor Statistics' *Occupational Outlook Handbook*, software developers usually need a bachelor's degree in computer science or software engineering. An internship at a software company while in college will help prepare you for this field. While software developers usually do not spend their entire workday writing code, they must have a background in computer programming. Software developers need to be able to analyze the needs of their users so that they can design software to fit those needs.

Being creative helps them come up with ideas. Communication skills help them with teamwork and dealing with customers. Being detail oriented, or concerned about getting every small detail correct, is important because computer code does only what you direct it to—it doesn't know how to account for your mistakes and typos. Lastly, problem-solving skills help software developers to overcome the challenges that they will face in bringing an idea to life in the physical world.

Software development has a bright future. The decade through 2026 will add 302,500 jobs, an increase of 24 percent, which is a much-faster rate than other jobs.

Computer programmers write and test code that produces software. They work with software developers and test newly developed applications to fix mistakes. They must have knowledge of a number of computer languages, such as Java and C++. Programmers often have a bachelor's degree in computer science and usually have expert knowledge in several programming languages. Important qualities of programmers are the ability to concentrate and be careful with details, since just one small mistake can mess up an entire program. Though computer programming can be a lucrative career, the Bureau of Labor Statistics states that in the decade ending in 2026, they project a 7 percent decline in the number of jobs available.

ARJUN KUMAR: A YOUNG APP INVENTOR

Arjun Kumar of Chennai, India, was only twelve years old when he won the 2012 MIT App Inventor International competition in the K–8 division. Arjun won for his app Ez School Bus Locator, which allows parents to use their smartphones to view the location of their child's school bus in real time, check to make sure their child is on the bus, and know how long it will take for the bus to arrive at its destination.

Arjun was inspired to create the app one day when heavy rain delayed his return home on the bus, which worried his parents. He researched online before choosing MIT App Inventor to develop his app. The source code for his app is available on the MIT App Inventor Gallery, and he has been contacted by other software developers to discuss his app. TechRepublic asked Arjun for advice for young people interested in app development. He said: "Look for problems around you, and get inspired from them. You'll see a lot of opportunities to use your (own) skills to make this world a better place to live!"

In the years since Arjun won the MIT App Inventor competition, he has gone on to form his own company, LateraLogics Innovations LLP, which works on apps and other technology to find solutions to real-world problems. One of the company's 2018 products, developed by Arjun himself, is ConnectKerala. The system connects relief workers and victims of a flood disaster in the Indian state of Kerala by pulling tweets from Twitter that use a hashtag such as #KeralaFloodRelief.

EDUCATIONAL GAMES AND APPS

In 2017, a report from App Annie, a market data firm, reported that users worldwide have downloaded 175 billion apps worth $86 billion. China has the most app users, followed by India and the United States in third place. Plenty of those are educational apps, such as those developed by the nonprofit online educator Khan Academy. Magoosh teaches vocabulary skills, English grammar, and math. Another example is iTooch Language Arts by eduPad (which also has games for many other subjects and for numerous grade levels).

In November 2016, *Minecraft: Education Edition* was released. An iPad version was released in fall 2018. The game impresses teachers with its uses. Not only does it help students work together, but it also nurtures creativity, reading and writing skills, problem-solving, and computer science knowledge. Coders—either in the classroom or on their own—can create and play by visiting the Code Builder section of the *Minecraft: Education Edition* website. Free materials teach users to code using ScratchX, Microsoft MakeCode, MakeCode, or Tynker, and mentors and a community forum help answer questions or assist users to overcome problems.

Microsoft Virtual Academy offers free online courses in game development, mobile app development, web development, and more. Udemy, Lynda, and other learning platforms also offer similar courses. Your local public library may subscribe to one of these services so that you can take classes tuition

Minecraft: Education Edition uses the game's fun features to teach students how to build code—and have fun at the same time.

free. One MOOC that offers a course entitled Design and Development of Games for Learning is edX. As with other MOOC offerings, this class is free but offers the option of adding a verified certificate for an extra fee. These classes provide the latest technology and allow you to learn and experiment without the pressure of an in-person course or coding boot camp.

Game development classes are popping up at universities all the time. If you are interested in a coding boot camp, check out Helio Training's Bootcamps, available online and in Salt Lake City, DaVinci Coders in Denver, Colorado, and iD Tech, geared toward students seven to eighteen years old and held in more than 150 locations worldwide.

If you would like to study on your own, find opportunities with Codesters (Python lessons), Gamestar Mechanic (online games and courses to teach game design), Adventure Time Game Wizard (an app that teaches basic game design), Scratch (a free programming language that teaches essential programming skills; available through MIT), Swift Playgrounds (an iPad app that teaches Swift code), and GameMaker Studio 2 (a multiplatform in-depth game design system).

In college, subjects include game design, computer science, and graphic design. Teamwork is usually important in this industry, so bolstering your team skills can help. Special skills for game designers include the creativity to develop stories that make the game come alive and the skills to build prototypes of games. Learning 3D modeling software like Maya can help make you stand apart and so can knowledge of the languages C++, Lua, and Python.

Employers include Microsoft, Zynga, Mattel, and more. This is a competitive field that is difficult to join, so you may want to look for smaller companies when you are beginning your career search so that you can gain experience.

LEARNING IN VIRTUAL REALITY

Virtual reality (VR) is a technology that immerses the viewer in a computerized world where he or she can move and react as if in the real world. It usually makes

Virtual reality makes use of eyewear and headsets to put users into a whole other digital world. While this can be done for fun, it also has many uses in education.

use of a device placed over the eyes (made by Oculus Rift, HTC Vive, or Monitor) all the while being in a 3D environment. In the classroom, students can use VR to interact and learn information. This can be done in the classroom by using web-based virtual tours that allow students to explore environments or objects. Or it could teach by enabling students to take a trip through the human circulatory system or by simulating combat in the military. Virtual reality also allows students to train on machinery without it existing there and then.

Examples of VR games are InMind 2, an action-based game that educates about the human brain; Titans of Space® that teaches about outer space; KingTut VR brings history to life with a VR rendering of King Tutankamun's tomb and objects related to it in the Egyptian Museum. Learn Languages VR helps students learn twenty-eight languages and had more than five hundred million downloads by April 2017. Google Cardboard encourages VR for everyone starting at low prices and even providing instructions about how to make the viewers.

If you want to work in VR, you will need to create some sample projects on your own through VR 3D platforms like Unity or Unreal. A background in C# or C++ is also important. Udemy has a number of online courses in VR, or the University of Idaho has an in-person bachelor's degree in virtual technology and design. Another option is to explore starting your own VR company. A Techstars Startup Weekend event can help you learn a lot about this option either online or in your own community.

OTHER JOBS IN EDUCATION

You may think that the only way you can use computer science skills in education is to work in traditional school systems or in companies that produce educational games, apps, or VR. That's not true, though. There are a range of jobs that combine coding with education, though they may not look like they do on the surface. State departments of education, nonprofits, libraries, museums, consultants, and private firms employ people as web developers, programmers, tech training specialists, and other positions. Let's look at a few of these.

IN THE LIBRARY

Library media specialists may be called by many names: school librarians, information specialists, computer services librarians, or information technologists. Such positions exist in public, private, and school libraries. They involve helping patrons and staff locate materials and access research. Specialists may obtain, design, and test programs to manage information needs and be responsible for library computer systems, software, and equipment.

The duties depend on the size of the library. Some librarians are responsible for creating and updating the library's website. They also work with teachers to find both print and digital teaching materials. Usually these positions require a master's degree and

Librarians are also media specialists who play a crucial role in today's schools and communities. They have been trained in research, much of which is computerized.

coursework in literature, computer science, and library and information science. Some school libraries may require teaching certificates.

AS A CONSULTANT

ESSDACK is a private company that works to help learners prepare for their future. They provide consultants for K–12 and postsecondary schools and organizations both in the United States and around the world. Glenn Wiebe from Hutchinson, Kansas, works for ESSDACK advising schools on how to integrate technology with their curriculum. In an interview with Teach.com, he says: "My primary focus is helping social studies teachers find ways to improve student learning. I also spend a lot of time with schools as they integrate [to unite as a whole] technology into instruction. The title on my business card is Curriculum and Technology Integration Specialist but I'm really just a guy who gets the chance to spend a lot of time with classroom teachers."

Wiebe taught eighth-grade history for nine years before spending time working at the college level. From there, he found a position as a consultant for ESSDACK where he looks for ways to bring technology into classrooms so that students have an easier time learning. He appreciates the more lax schedule of a consultant since teachers often have little time for lunch and breaks. He also enjoys working with teachers to find ways to help students. ESSDACK is just one of many private firms that employ educators in a computer science role.

TESTING WHIZZES

Psychometricians are highly skilled professionals in the science of measuring learners' knowledge and skills. They develop computerized assessments, often for educational companies and state departments of education. In addition to creating test questions that accurately assess students' knowledge, they use computer programs to analyze data analysis, score tests, and produce complex reports about a state's population of students.

They usually work for private firms that contract with state governments and other organizations. This position often requires advanced education, such as a master's degree in quantitative psychology. Employers can include places like the New York State Education Department, where the state education psychometrician works on helping low-performing schools to increase their test scores. Many staff members support psychometricians, including analysts and assistants. Each position can include sophisticated computer modeling, data development and layout, and other types of analysis using statistics.

These are just a few of the many jobs that combine computer science and education. The field is changing and growing with each coming year. If your passion lies in coding and education, now is the best time to start learning the skills that can make your dreams a reality.

GLOSSARY

accredited A course of study that is officially recognized.

algorithm A step-by-step method of problem solving.

attribute A quality that belongs to a certain person or thing.

charter An independent school established by community groups, teachers, or parents under a charter.

cloud computing The use of the internet to store and process data instead of it being confined to a personal computer or dedicated network.

collaborate To work together.

credentials Documents that prove that a person can perform certain tasks.

cryptographer A person who breaks codes or encrypted messages.

curriculum A roster of lessons and other information taught in schools.

expertise Skill belonging to an expert.

gameification Using certain elements of games, like point scoring, to draw people to use a product or service.

literacy Competence in a certain area.

loop The repetition of a series of instructions.

open source Software in which the original source code is made freely available to be changed and redistributed.

postsecondary Education beyond the high school level.

proactive Having to do with actions that anticipate future changes, problems, or needs.

psychometrics The study of psychological measurement in education.

punch card A card with holes that was once used to control the operation of a machine.

rubric A guide that shows the requirements for scoring schoolwork.

sophisticated Complex.

specialized Skilled at one subject or area of study.

tedious Dull and tiring.

transistor An electronic device made of semiconductors, with electrodes that control the flow of electricity in electronic equipment such as computers.

tuition Money paid to a school for instruction.

Boys & Girls Clubs of America National Headquarters
1275 Peachtree Street NE
Atlanta, GA 30309-3506
(404) 487-5700
Website: https://www.bgca.org
Facebook: @bgca.clubs
Twitter and Instagram: @bgca_clubs
More than 4,300 clubs across the United States serve about four million young people every year. They offer a range of programs, including sports, leadership, the arts, and technology such as the Computer Science Pathway, which emphasizes STEM programming.

Canada's Association of Information Technology Professionals (CIPS) National Office
1375 Southdown Road, Unit 16, Suite 802
Mississauga, ON L5J 2Z1
Canada
(905) 602-1370
(877) ASK-CIPS (275-2477)
Website: http://www.cips.ca
Facebook: @CIPS.ca
CIPS offers networking opportunities, certification of IT professionals (ISP and ITCP designations), accreditation of IT university and college programs, and an IT job board.

Code.org
1501 4th Avenue, Suite 900
Seattle, WA 98101
Website: https://code.org
Facebook: @Code.org
Twitter and Instagram: @codeorg
A nonprofit organization, Code.org is dedicated to "expanding access to computer science in schools and increasing participation by women and underrepresented minorities." They offer a number of coding courses for grades K–12 and beyond and sponsor the Hour of Code event.

Codecademy
575 Broadway, 5th Floor
New York, NY 10012
Website: https://www.codecademy.com
Facebook, Twitter, and Instagram: @codecademy
This education company teaches coding courses to millions. It offers both free and paid options.

Esri Developer Summit
380 New York Street
Redlands, CA
(888) 377-4576
Email: devsummit@esri.com
Website: https://www.esri.com/en-us/about/events devsummit/overview
Facebook and Twitter: @esridevsummit
Instagram: @esrigram
This yearly conference in Palm Springs, California, is designed to teach students, teachers, and

other users how to create cutting-edge apps with advanced GIS mapping technology.

iNACOL
1934 Old Gallows Road, Suite 350
Vienna, VA 22182-4040
(888) 956-2265
Website: https://www.inacol.org
Facebook: @inacol
Twitter: @nacol
iNACOL, International Association for K–12 Online Learning, provides resources for educators who teach online, including national quality standards.

FOR FURTHER READING

Bedell, Jane (J. M.). *So, You Want to Be a Coder?* New York, NY: Simon & Schuster, 2016.

Beedie, Duncan. *Get Coding! Learn HTML, CSS, and JavaScript and Build a Website, App, and Game*. Somerville, MA: Candlewick Press, 2017.

Heitkamp, Kristina Lyn. *Getting Paid to Make Games and Apps*. New York, NY: Rosen Publishing, 2017.

Kassnoff, David. *What Degree Do I Need to Pursue a Career in Information Technology & Information Systems?* New York, NY: Rosen Publishing, 2015.

Mara, Wil. *Software Development*. New York, NY: Scholastic, Inc., 2016.

Matthes, Eric. *Python Crash Course: A Hands-On, Project-Based Introduction to Programming*. San Francisco, CA: No Starch Press, 2015.

McKinney, Devon. *A Day at Work with a Software Developer*. New York, NY: PowerKids Press, 2016.

Saujani, Reshma. *Girls Who Code: Learn to Code and Change the World.* New York, NY: Viking, 2017.

Sheen, Barbara. *Careers in Education*. San Diego, CA: ReferencePoint Press, 2016.

Sweigart, Al. *Cracking Codes with Python: An Introduction to Building and Breaking Ciphers.* San Francisco, CA: No Starch Press, 2018.

Audacity. "Plug-Ins | Audacity®." Retrieved October 15, 2018. http://www.audacityteam.org/download/plug-ins.

Bedell, Jane (J. M.). *So, You Want to Be a Coder?* New York, NY: Simon & Schuster, 2016.

Biography.com editors. "Ada Lovelace Biography." October 10, 2018. http://www.biography.com/people/ada-lovelace-20825323.

BlendedLearningToolkit. "What Is Blended Learning?" March 12, 2015. http://blended.online.ucf.edu/about/what-is-blended-learning.

Boys & Girls Clubs of America. "BGCA - FAQs." Retrieved October 15, 2018. http://www.bgca.org/about-us/faqs#one.

Casky, Jack. "Interview with a Location Independent Online English Teacher." YouTube, Teachingeslonline, January 22, 2015. http://www.youtube.com/watch?v=lcvLr8USnQ4.

ClassDojo. "ClassDojo Toolkit." Retrieved October 15, 2018. http://www.classdojo.com/toolkit.

Community for Accredited Online Schools. "Online Elementary School | Decide the Right Fit for Your Child." Retrieved October 15, 2018. http://www.accreditedschoolsonline.org/k-12/online-elementary -school/#Is-Online-Elementary-School-Right-for-Your-Child?.

ConnectKerala. "About." Retrieved October 15, 2018. connectkerala2018.firebaseapp.com/about.html.

Davis, Vicki. "A Guidebook for Social Media in the Classroom." Edutopia, George Lucas Educational

Foundation, February 19, 2015. http://www.edutopia.org/blog/guidebook-social-media-in-classroom-vicki-davis.

Edgenuity Inc. "America's Education Technology Gap." August 28, 2018. http://www.edgenuity.com/americas-education-technology-gap.

Education Dive. "As Blended Learning Grows, Students Demand More Face Time with Professors." OLC, September 25, 2018. http://onlinelearningconsortium.org/news_item/as-blended-learning-grows-students-demand-more-face-time-with-professors.

Forbes. "What Skills Do Game Designers Need?" September 1, 2017. http://www.forbes.com.

Francis, William J. "Interview with 13-Year-Old MIT App Inventor Winner Arjun Kumar." TechRepublic, October 16, 2013. www.techrepublic.com/blog/software-engineer/interview-with-13-year-old-mit-app-inventor-winner-arjun-kumar.

FutureLearn. "Our Story." Retrieved October 15, 2018. http://www.futurelearn.com/about-futurelearn.

GeoInquiries American Literature. "Esri GeoInquiries™ for American Literature." Retrieved October 15, 2018. http://www.esri.com/en-us/industries/education/schools/geoinquiries-american-literature.

GeoInquiries Mathematics. "Esri GeoInquiries™ for Mathematics." Retrieved October 15, 2018. http://www.esri.com/en-http://us/industries/education/schools/geoinquiries-mathematics.

Get In Media. "Game Designer." Retrieved October 15, 2018. http://getinmedia.com/careers/game-designer.

Glassdoor. "State Education Psychometrician." September 5, 2018. http://www.glassdoor.com.

Google Expeditions. "McGuffey Middle School Story | Google for Education." Retrieved October 15, 2018. http://edu.google.com.

Growth of K–12 Online Education Infographic. "Career FAQs." Retrieved October 15, 2018. http://www.connectionsacademy.com/careers/faqs.

Hunter, Adrienne. "How to Get a Job in VR – Virtual Reality Pop." Virtual Reality Pop, November 29, 2016. http://virtualrealitypop.com/how-to-get-a-job-in-vr-fff5c9d56a13.

Instructional Tech Talk. "What Is EdTech?" February 12, 2016. http://instructionaltechtalk.com/what-is-edtech.

Ioffe, Yevgeny. "Q&A With Jack Macleod, President of Alma |." EdTech Times, February 25, 2015. http://edtechtimes.com/2015/02/26/qa-jack-macleod-president-alma.

Jones, Barbara A. "Los Angeles Unified School District." Retrieved October 15, 2018. http://achieve.lausd.net.

Minecraft: Education Edition. "How Minecraft Impacts Classrooms." Retrieved October 15, 2018. http://education.minecraft.net/impact.

Minecraft Wiki. "Education Edition." Gamepedia, September 29, 2018. http://minecraft.gamepedia.com/Education_Edition.

National Center for Education Statistics (NCES). "Digest of Education Statistics, 2017." US Department of Educatio. Retrieved October 15, 2018. http://nces.ed.gov/programs/digest/d17

/tables/dt17_218.40.asp?current=yes.

National Center for Education Statistics. "Educational Technology in U.S. Public Schools: Fall 2008." US Department of Education, April 2010. http://nces.ed.gov/pubs2010/2010034.pdf.

Peterson, Deb. "Is Taking a Massive Open Online Course, or MOOC, a Good or Bad Thing?" ThoughtCo., March 8, 2017. http://www.thoughtco.com/the-pros-and-cons-of-moocs-31030.

Petkov, Alexander. "Here Are the Best Programming Languages to Learn in 2018." FreeCodeCamp.org, January 16, 2018. http://medium.freecodecamp.org/best-programming-languages-to-learn-in-2018-ultimate-guide-bfc93e615b35.

Prof Testing. "What Is a Psychometrician?" Retrieved October 15, 2018. http://www.proftesting.com/test_topics/pdfs/psychometrician.pdf.

Research Guides: University of Wisconsin-Madison Libraries. "Research Guides: Mapping and Geographic Information Systems (GIS): What Is GIS?" Retrieved October 15, 2018. https://researchguides.library.wisc.edu/GIS.

Ruiz, Liz. Programmer analyst, LAUSD, interview by Xina M. Uhl, September 21, 2018.

Saujani, Reshma. *Girls Who Code: Learn to Code and Change the World.* New York, NY: Viking, 2017.

Snyder, Thomas D., et al. "Digest of Education Statistics 2016." IES National Center for Education Statistics, February 2018. http://nces.ed.gov/pubs2017/2017094.pdf.

Stiffler, Brian. Music educator, interview by Xina M. Uhl, September 28, 2018.

SwitchUp. "How to Learn Game Design - Best Bootcamps and Courses." July 16, 2017. http://www.switchup.org/subjects/how-to-learn-game-design.

Teach: Make a Difference. "From Teacher to Curriculum Specialist: 8 Questions with Glenn Wiebe." August 24, 2015.

Teach: Make a Difference. "How to Become a School Administrator." Retrieved October 15, 2018. http://teach.com/become/other-education-careers/school-admin.

Techopedia.com. "What Is a Database (DB)? - Definition from Techopedia." Retrieved October 15, 2018. http://www.techopedia.com/definition/1185/database-db.

Techopedia.com. "What Is Computer Science? - Definition from Techopedia." Retrieved October 15, 2018. http://www.techopedia.com/definition/592/computer-science.

Tucker, Bill. "The Flipped Classroom." *Education Next*, September 12, 2017. http://www.educationnext.org/the-flipped-classroom.

University of Maryland Department of Computer Science. "What Is Computer Science?" Retrieved October 15, 2018. http://undergrad.cs.umd.edu/what-computer-science.

US Bureau of Labor Statistics. "Education, Training, and Library Occupations." April 13, 2018. http://www.bls.gov/ooh/education-training-and-library/home.htm.

US Bureau of Labor Statistics. "Elementary, Middle, and High School Principals." April 13, 2018. http://

www.bls.gov/ooh/management/elementary-middle-and-high-school-principals.htm#tab-1.

US Bureau of Labor Statistics. "High School Teachers." *Occupational Outlook Handbook*, April 13, 2018. http://www.bls.gov/ooh/education-training-and-library/high-school-teachers.htm.

US Bureau of Labor Statistics. "How to Become a Computer Programmer." US Bureau of Labor Statistics, April 13, 2018. http://www.bls.gov/ooh/computer-and-information-technology/computer-programmers.htm#tab-4.

US Bureau of Labor Statistics. "How to Become a Middle School Teacher." *Occupational Outlook Handbook*, April 13, 2018. http://www.bls.gov/ooh/education-training-and-library/middle-school-teachers.htm#tab-4.

US Bureau of Labor Statistics. "How to Become a Postsecondary Teacher." *Occupational Outlook Handbook*, April 13, 2018. http://www.bls.gov/ooh/education-training-and-library/postsecondary-teachers.htm#tab-4.

US Bureau of Labor Statistics. "How to Become a Software Developer." April 13, 2018. http://www.bls.gov/ooh/computer-and-information-technology/software-developers.htm#tab-4.

US Bureau of Labor Statistics. "Kindergarten and Elementary School Teachers." Occupatio*nal* Outlook Handbook, April 13, 2018. http://www.bls.gov/ooh/education-training-and-library/kindergarten-and-elementary-school-teachers.htm.

US Bureau of Labor Statistics. "Middle School Teachers." *Occupational Outlook Handbook*, April

13, 2018. http://www.bls.gov/ooh/education -training-and-library/middle-school-teachers.htm.

US Bureau of Labor Statistics. "Postsecondary Teachers." *Occupational Outlook Handbook*, April 13, 2018. http://www.bls.gov/ooh/education -training-and-library/postsecondary-teachers .htm#tab-1.

US Bureau of Labor Statistics. "Summary: Software Developers." April 13, 2018. http://www.bls.gov /ooh/computer-and-information-technology /software-developers.htm#tab-1.

Vandewater, Cathy. "From Teacher to Tech-Savvy Principal: 8 Questions with Jeff Herb." Teach: Make a Difference, July 13, 2015. http://teach.com /blog/jeff-herb.

White House, The. "Presidential Memorandum for the Secretary of Education." September 25, 2017. http://www.whitehouse.gov/presidential-actions /presidential-memorandum-secretary-education.

White House, The. "President Trump Signs Presidential Memo to Increase Access to STEM and Computer Science Education." September 25, 2017. http:// www.whitehouse.gov/articles /president-trump-signs-presidential-memo-increase -access-stem-computer-science-education.

Zimmerman, Eli. "5 Key Areas of Technology Professional Development for Teachers." *EdTech*, Focus on K–12, September 14, 2018. http:// edtechmagazine.com.

INDEX

ABOUT THE AUTHOR

Xina M. Uhl has written numerous educational books for young people and maintains a passion for learning. She has tackled subjects including history, biographies, technology, and health concerns. Visit her blog for details about her travels, publications, book reviews, and the occasional cat picture.

PHOTO CREDITS

Cover Tanya Constantine/Blend Images/Getty Images; back cover, pp. 4–5 (background) nadla/E+/Getty Images; p. 5 (inset) © iStockphoto.com/Daviles; pp. 7, 16, 30, 42, 52 (background) panitanphoto/Shutterstock.com, (circuit pattern) Titima Ongkantong/Shutterstock.com; p. 8 Vintage Tone/Shutterstock.com; p. 9 EThamPhoto/Corbis Documentary/Getty Images; p. 14 Caiaimage/Robert Daly/Getty Images; p. 17 vgajic/E+/Getty Images; p. 21 © AP Images; p. 25 Sharaf Maksumov/Shutterstock.com; p. 27 dennizn/Shutterstock.com; p. 31 Africa Studio/Shutterstock.com; p. 33 ZUMA Press Inc./Alamy Stock Photo; pp. 38–39 PeopleImages/E+/Getty Images; p. 40 Piotr Swat/Shutterstock.com; p. 43 adamkaz/E+/Getty Images; p. 45 Steve Debenport/E+/Getty Images; p. 48 Boston Globe/Getty Images; p. 53 Rawpixel.com/Shutterstock.com; p. 57 AP Images for Microsoft; p. 59 LightField Studios/Shutterstock.com; p. 62 Jupiterimages/Stockbyte/Getty Images; additional background textures and graphics Verticalarray/Shutterstock.com (p. 1), Toria/Shutterstock.com (p. 3).

Design: Michael Moy; Layout: Nicole Russo-Duca; Photo Researcher: Karen Huang